BATH

Text by
PAUL NEWMAN

Photographs by
ERNEST FRANKL

PEVENSEY
Heritage Guides

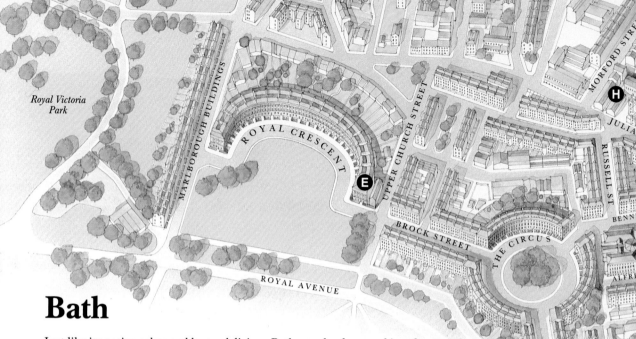

Bath

Just like its native cakes and buns, delicious Bath may be devoured in a few greedy bites, or elegantly nibbled and gently savoured. That is the best way to do it, to stroll its streets and allow its many flavours, matured over a millennium or two, to permeate. It is a city that has been much loved and given much pleasure in return, a city of grace and wit, whose earlier inhabitants seem more reluctant to leave than those of other places. Certainly, it would be a difficult place for a ghost to quit, whether he were the old Roman cavalryman whose tomb can be seen in the Temple of Sulis-Minerva, the merry Bishop King who built the abbey, or the Woods, father and son, who laboured with such restrained passion upon the incomparable Georgian streets, circus and crescent.

Jane Austen, too, would be happy to see that the shops in Bond Street are as suave as ever, Sally Lunn that her buns are finding as ready a market, and Sir Thomas Holburne to see that his collections are appreciated by later generations. And surely those two spirits of the Pump Room, Beau Nash and Dr Oliver, still drift among the tea tables, one proffering the latest gossip, and the other his healthful biscuits.

PLACES TO SEE

Ⓐ Bath Abbey
All year, Mon-Sat. Free entry.
Tel (0225) 330289

Ⓑ Roman Baths and Museum
About 20ft below modern Bath there lies the Roman spa and holiday resort of Aquae Sulis. Its most splendid feature was the Great Bath, a roofed-in warm pool, 70ft long, 30ft wide and 5ft deep, constantly fed by the hot spring enclosed in an adjoining reservoir. It was overlooked by the Temple of Sulis-Minerva – a joint dedication to the Celtic and Roman goddesses of healing.

The museum wanders out and in of the modern city. The Great Bath is in the open air, but the spring that feeds it lies beneath what is now the King's Bath.
All year, daily. Adm charge.
Tel (0225) 461111 extn 2785.

Ⓒ Pump Room
The present Pump Room dates from the very end of the 18th century, when Bath was booming and the old room was becoming too small to accommodate all the people who came to imbibe the prescribed five daily glasses of the local fluid and remained to gossip.

The floor of the Pump Room is dotted with round tables clad in immaculate linen, at which visitors may take morning coffee or afternoon tea and nibble on a Sally Lunn bun to the accompaniment of the pump Room Trio. A little fountain provides glasses of The Water – tasting, as Dickens's Sam Weller described it, of 'warm flat irons'.
All year, daily, Free entry. Tel (0225) 461111 extn 2785.

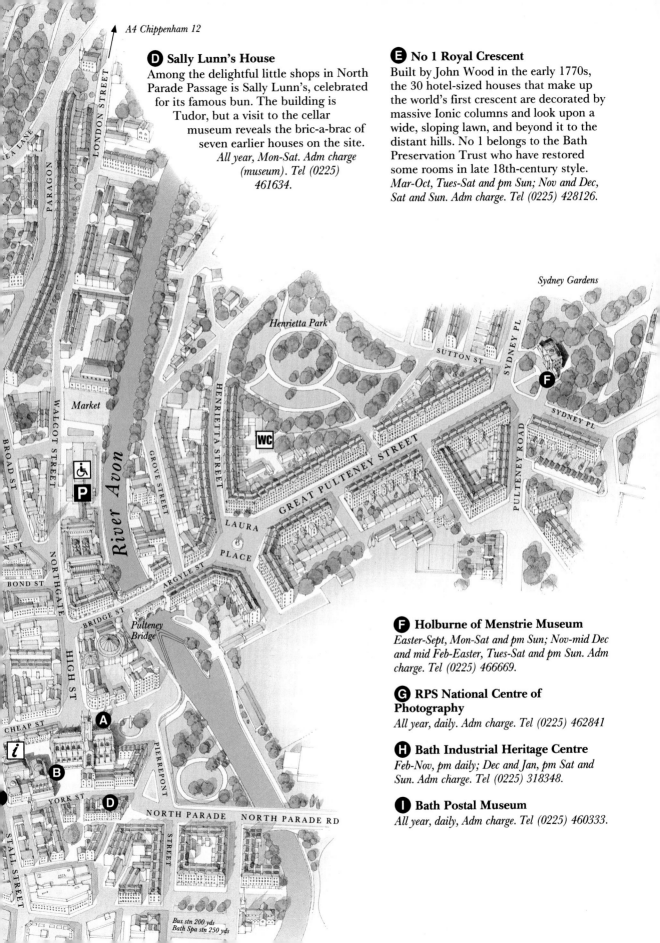

A4 Chippenham 12

D Sally Lunn's House
Among the delightful little shops in North Parade Passage is Sally Lunn's, celebrated for its famous bun. The building is Tudor, but a visit to the cellar museum reveals the bric-a-brac of seven earlier houses on the site.
All year, Mon-Sat. Adm charge (museum). Tel (0225) 461634.

E No 1 Royal Crescent
Built by John Wood in the early 1770s, the 30 hotel-sized houses that make up the world's first crescent are decorated by massive Ionic columns and look upon a wide, sloping lawn, and beyond it to the distant hills. No 1 belongs to the Bath Preservation Trust who have restored some rooms in late 18th-century style.
Mar-Oct, Tues-Sat and pm Sun; Nov and Dec, Sat and Sun. Adm charge. Tel (0225) 428126.

F Holburne of Menstrie Museum
Easter-Sept, Mon-Sat and pm Sun; Nov-mid Dec and mid Feb-Easter, Tues-Sat and pm Sun. Adm charge. Tel (0225) 466669.

G RPS National Centre of Photography
All year, daily. Adm charge. Tel (0225) 462841

H Bath Industrial Heritage Centre
Feb-Nov, pm daily; Dec and Jan, pm Sat and Sun. Adm charge. Tel (0225) 318348.

I Bath Postal Museum
All year, daily, Adm charge. Tel (0225) 460333.

Bus stn 200 yds
Bath Spa stn 250 yds

A Pevensey Heritage Guide

First published 1986
Reprinted 1987, 1988, 1990
Revised Edition 1993
Reprinted 1996

Photographs: Ernest Frankl, except p.8: Bath Museum Service; p.21: Victoria Art Gallery, Bath; pp.70–1:
Cambridge University Collection of Aerial Photographs; p.85: The American Museum in Britain,
Claverton Manor; p.91: Victoria Art Gallery, Bath, and (portrait of Jane Austen) J. Butler Kearney

Colour map copyright © The Reader's Digest Association Ltd
Inside back cover map by Vincent Driver

The assistance of Dr Brigitte Mitchell is gratefully acknowledged

A catalogue record for this book is available from the British Library.

ISBN 0 907115 59 4

Design by Book Production Consultants, Cambridge
Printed in Hong Kong by Wing King Tong Co. Ltd
for David & Charles plc
Brunel House Newton Abbot Devon

The Pevensey Press is an imprint of David & Charles plc

Front cover
Lansdown Crescent

Back cover
The Great Bath and the south-west angle of the Abbey; Queen Street and Trim Bridge;
Margaret's Buildings

Title page inset
Fan-vaulting in the Abbey

Contents

History

Most English towns have developed haphazardly. Successive generations have altered and added to existing structures, each leaving some distinctive mark, and the result is the mixture of styles that makes sightseeing such a rewarding pastime. Bath gives a different impression. Although its history dates from the 1st century, its present form did not emerge piecemeal. More than any other city in England, it was planned in accordance with a coherent vision inspired by commitment to a particular architectural style, and when we admire the beauty of the Georgian squares, crescents and terraces, we are responding to a calculated effect, not to the sort of happy visual accident that occurs when we catch sight of York Minster closing the view up Stonegate, or see the backs of the colleges from the river at Cambridge. To a quite unusual degree, Bath conveys a sense of harmonious unity.

Roman and Saxon foundations

The image of present-day Bath was forged in the 18th century; but the site was first developed by the Romans, shortly after they came to Britain in AD 43. One of their most important roads, the Fosse Way, linking East Anglia and the West Country, forded the River Avon at Bath, and here there was probably a small garrison – tombstones have been found of soldiers who perhaps died on frontier duty. The place had a particular advantage. Beside the Avon meadows was a soft expanse of ground which, unlike other marshy patches, was not unpleasantly cold and slimy, but fed by a gushing hot spring that stained the rocks red and invigorated the body of anyone who bathed in it. There was also rich agricultural land, and the wealth of Mendip tin and lead close at hand.

The spring seemed like a gift from the gods to the soldiers. They had been posted from a balmy land of olive trees and vines to the bleakest outpost of progress – a misty island pounded by moody seas, with an interior of wolf-infested forests occupied by painted people who practised alien rites. But so long as local beliefs were not militant, the Romans were willing to incorporate them, adapting and transforming them for their own purposes. So when they found that the miraculous spring near the Avon was sacred to Sulis, they decided to link this local Celtic deity to a Roman goddess associated with health and healing, and build a temple in their joint honour above the sacred spring. The four fluted Corinthian columns of the imposing façade were raised, and surmounted by a pediment: elaborately carved with helmets, winged victories and tritons, its centrepiece was a shield bearing a male Gorgon's head, heavily moustachioed, with staring eyes. This was Sulis, whose chosen Roman consort was Minerva, goddess of healing and wisdom, to whom springs and streams were sacred. Images of both deities can be seen in the Roman Baths Museum near the spot where they were formerly venerated.

Each day in Bath 250,000 gallons of water rush from underground at a temperature of 46.5°C. This is the overflow from the Romans' sacred spring and reservoir into the outfall drain, which led to the river.

Sulis and the springs gave Bath its Roman name – Aquae Sulis. The hot water was piped and channelled into a series of capacious baths, sealed with layers of lead and enclosed by a paved colonnade (see pp. 28–31). Around them a splendid resort arose, with public buildings of the kind that later inspired Bath's Georgian architects. The temple became the focus of a precinct which included a sacrificial altar, the monumental entrance to the spring, and numerous dedications, all surrounded by a portico. Besides the temple and baths at the principal spring (where the Great Bath and King's Bath are now), there was

a bath on the site of the Hot Bath spring, a shrine where the Cross Bath was later built, and structures on a grand scale in the area of the Abbey and Abbey Church Yard (perhaps a theatre or forum) and Westgate Street. Defensive walls (3rd–4th centuries) probably surrounded the central area (their line served as a building boundary until the 18th century), but the Roman town extended beyond them – there was a sizeable suburb at Walcot.

The Romans stayed for nearly four hundred years, but in 410, the emperor Honorius told the people of Britain that Rome was no longer able to assist them against the marauding Picts, Scots, Saxons and Franks. Alaric the Goth was marching on Rome and all the garrisons were to be recalled. At this period the famous war leader afterwards called King Arthur beat back the invaders with his highly skilled cavalrymen, and at some time between 490 and 518 he won a

The carving from the centre of the pediment surmounting the main front of the Roman temple of Sulis-Minerva – a conflation of a classical Gorgon and the native Celtic deity, Sulis.

8

great victory at a place called Mons Badonicus, which is often identified as Bath.

The magnificent complex of baths rapidly fell into disrepair. The plumbing and the outfalls became choked with mud and slime. Pondweeds colonised the stagnating water, and much of the masonry crumbled and collapsed. The Saxon invaders had been used to living in wattle and daub huts, and the concept of drains, let alone regular immersion in warm water, was utterly alien to them. After the Battle of Dyrham in 577 the settlement had become a frontier post of the invading Saxon armies under Ceawlin – an important foothold in the Avon valley from which they could drive westward and complete the conquest. Further information is gleaned from Saxon charters, sometimes forged to reinforce oral tradition, but also containing vital matter. In 676 it is recorded that Osric, who acted as deputy king of Mercia, granted to the Abbess Bertana a large area of land for the erection and endowment of a monastery of holy virgins. Another reference to this foundation occurs around 681, when a man named Athelmod donated to it some property on the Cherwell. By 758 it appears to have been superseded by a monastery of monks dedicated to St Peter. This monastery was described in a charter of King Edwy of 957 as being of 'wondrous workmanship' (*mira fabrica constructum*), and additional grants are recorded 'to St Peter the Apostle and the venerable family of Bath'.

At this period St Dunstan was beginning to make his mark, first as Abbot of Glastonbury and later as Archbishop of Canterbury, attempting to bring the English church into line with the ascetic rule of the Benedictines. It was he who presided over the coronation of the young King Edgar in Bath in 973 and performed the anointing rite. A near-contemporary account describes two bishops leading the prince to the church, one on either side, chanting the antiphon. Edgar was wearing his crown, but laid it aside on reaching the high altar. Dunstan began singing the Te Deum, and was joined by the multitude of monks and clergy. Next Edgar, under the archbishop's direction, took the threefold oath: To guard the church of God; to forbid violence and wrong; to keep justice, judgement and mercy. He was then anointed, a ring was placed on his hand and the crown on his head, and he received the sceptre and rod. The coronation was by far the most important event to have touched the town since the Roman occupation, and was celebrated each Whitsuntide for hundreds of years afterwards. In the 16th century the antiquarian John Leland commented:

> King Eadgar was crounid with much joy and honor at St Peter's in Bath: wheraupon he bare a gret zeale to the towne, and gave very great frauncheses and privileges onto it. In the knowlege wherof they pray in al their ceremonies for the soule of King Eadgar. And at Whitsunday-tyde, at the which tyme men say that Eadgar there was crounid, ther is a king electid at Bath every yere of the tounes men in the joyfulle remembraunce of King Edgar and the privileges gyven to the toun by hym. This king is festid and his adherentes, by the richest menne of the toun.

Saxon Bath was virtually ruled by the Benedictine monks, who had incorporated the hot springs within their monastic buildings. But its importance was more than ecclesiastical, for it lay on the border of the powerful kingdoms of Mercia and Wessex. The River Avon traced the demarcation, and the Saxon kings favoured Bath as neutral territory where they could draw up charters, formulate peace treaties and discuss impending developments. It also had economic strength, being on major trade routes, and was the site of a palace and a royal mint. But these assets also made it vulnerable. An ancient tradition states that Alfred the Great restored the old Roman walls during the Danish attacks of the 9th century, and the Anglo-Saxon Chronicle records that in 1012 Sweyn, King of Denmark, attacked and took hostages.

Medieval turmoils

Strife continued even after the Norman Conquest. In 1088 the town was partly destroyed by Robert de Mowbray, an enemy of King William Rufus. The king, on the advice of Archbishop Lanfranc, conferred the see of Bath on Jean de Villula of Tours, a church dignitary who was also an outstanding physician. In deference to the Roman tradition he began building massively in stone, first a capacious cathedral church, then an imposing residence for himself called the Bishop's Bower. He probably repaired the medicinal springs, and the King's Bath may take its name from his royal patron. The splendid new church was destroyed by fire in 1137, during the civil wars which vexed King Stephen's reign, but was subsequently restored by a supporter of the king, the historian Bishop Robert of Lewes. In Robert's anonymous chronicle Gesta Stephani, Bath features as

> . . . a city where little springs through hidden conduits send up waters heated without human skills or ingenuity from deep in the bowels of the earth to a basin vaulted over with noble arches, creating in the middle of the town baths of agreeable warmth . . . the sick are wont to gather there from all England to wash away their infirmities in the health-giving waters, and the whole to see the wondrous jets of water and bathe in them.

It was to enable the poor and sick of the city to benefit from the waters that Bishop Reginald (Bishop of Bath 1174–91) founded Bath's oldest charitable institution, St John's Hospital, under the management of Augustinian monks. Its buildings have had a chequered history, but the charity is still in existence, on its original site (see p. 50).

During the reign of King John (1199–1216), the monastery declined and was ruthlessly plundered. By 1213 the monks were forced to subsist on gifts made to them by Ralph de Lechdale, canon of the splendid new cathedral at Wells. This was now the seat of the bishops and the headquarters of the episcopal see, and the numbers of monks at Bath show the abbey's lessening importance: forty in 1205, thirty in 1344, and after the Black Death (1349), twenty-two. Jean de Villula's lofty church (the present Abbey occupies only the area of its nave) was in decay, and so, it seems, was law and order. When Henry VI visited Bath in 1449, he was dismayed by the custom of stealing bathers' clothing and only returning it after ransom money had been paid.

Tudor and Stuart growth

Reforms were inaugurated in 1499 by Bishop Oliver King. The manner in which the present Abbey was conceived is depicted on its west front, which records a dream, or vision, seen by the bishop shortly after he had been wandering amidst the gaunt skeleton of de Villula's once-glorious edifice. He saw the Holy Trinity and a ladder with angels ascending and descending. At the foot of the ladder was an olive tree, crowned. A voice pierced the vision, saying 'Let an olive establish the crown and a king restore the church.' He took the

The west doors of the Abbey, donated in 1617 by Sir Henry Montague, brother of the bishop, are richly carved as a single composition of shields, drapery, cartouches and the helmet of a knight. Above the arch the spandrels of the doorway are carved with the instruments of the Passion. The statue above is of Henry VII, during whose reign the present Abbey was begun – this sculpture is Victorian, but the statues on either side of the door are early 16th century.

10

imagery and language to be a direct play on his name, and split the revenue of the monastery, allowing £180 for the subsistence of the prior and monks and £300 for rebuilding the church. And he appointed William Birde as prior, to implement the vision.

The old structure was in such bad condition that it needed renewal rather than repair. Prior Birde planned an entirely new church in the Perpendicular style, and what we see today is the outcome of that plan; but he died in 1525, leaving the completion of the work to his successor, William Holleway. No sooner had the project been accomplished than the accession of Henry VIII imperilled it. Even before the Dissolution, the king sent his agent Dr Richard Layton to Bath to collect material for his 'Black Book' of charges against the clergy. Layton asserted that Holleway was an upright man but 'simple and not of the greatest wit' – whereas other contemporaries praised his learning. As for the monks, Layton reported that one of them had ten mistresses, some of them eight, and all the rest 'no fewer'. The statement is almost funny in its outrageous cynicism – any old lie would suffice. Prior Holleway was dismissed in 1539, and he received a good pension of £80 a year, but ultimately he lost his reason and died blind and insane. Prior Birde, however, is commemorated in the Abbey by his chantry chapel (1515), which has a beautiful fan-vaulted ceiling and is adorned with canopied niches and sculptured and fretted screens. His escutcheon is mounted on the semi-vault at the east end.

When John Leland visited Bath in the 1540s, the town was essentially a medieval cloth centre with three main entrance gates (to north, south and west); the thoroughfares were cart-rutted and broken by numerous boggy patches. He inspected the baths, and reported that in all three 'a man may evidently se how the water burbelith up from the springes'. There was a fives court beyond the town walls, a cock pit in Timber Green and two bowling greens. Leland evoked the roofless ruins of Jean de Villula's church, with weeds infesting the stately tomb of the founder, and referred to the 'right goodly new church' at the west end. Yet this too was on the verge of decay. At the Dissolution the Abbey was offered to the citizens of Bath for a mere 500 marks, but they refused to take it, and the building was stripped of its lead, glass and bells. It passed into private hands but continued to deteriorate until 1568, when Edmund Colthurst, then the owner, gave it to the city. When Queen Elizabeth visited Bath in 1574, its outer walls were so disfigured that the council had them concealed with evergreens. Choristers were brought over from Wells and rubbish was cleared from the city gates to honour the occasion. The queen was touched with concern at the sight of the mouldering Abbey and launched a national appeal which enabled Bishop Montague, in 1609, to roof the choir and restore parts of the building.

During the Civil War, Bath served as both a Roundhead and a Cavalier base. The town itself escaped destruction at this time, partly because it was represented in Parliament by the extreme Puritan William Prynne; but there was one notable battle, on Lansdown Hill in 1643, when Sir Bevil Grenville fell after leading his pikemen against Cromwell's troops. This was the last occasion on which Bath experienced armed conflict, until it was bombed during World War II.

Contemporary reports suggest that life in Tudor and Stuart Bath, far from restoring health to invalids, required a tough constitution. In 1590 Queen Elizabeth issued a charter confirming all the town's ancient rights, but at the same time she expressed strong disapproval of the smell of its streets. Her

Looking across Orange Grove to the north-east side of the Abbey. There are three obelisks in Bath, commemorating royal visits; this one was commissioned from John Wood the elder by Beau Nash in honour of Prince William of Orange, who came to Bath in 1734, the year in which he married one of the daughters of George II.

reservations are echoed by the diarist John Evelyn, who (following the growing fashion) visited Bath in 1654: 'I bathed in the Crosse Bathe . . . The King's Bath is esteemed ye fairest in Europe. The toune is entirely built of stone, but the streetes narrow, uneven and unpleasant.' Samuel Pepys, visiting in 1688, was less fastidious: he found the town 'most of stone, and clean, though the streets generally narrow', and admired the 'very fine ladies' who shared the baths with him. The previous year the intrepid traveller Celia Fiennes had described the town as almost exclusively 'adapted to the bath and drinking of waters'. She detected in the water the flavour of sulphur, 'like the water that boils eggs', and observed the unpleasant mantle of scum (which tended to produce pimples and heat rashes) being raked off the bathwater each day. The image of marbled Roman splendour surrounding the baths was created by the Georgians. During

13

the Stuart period changing facilities were limited to passageways, where clothes were deposited and the rough walls were encrusted with dirt and slime. A picture exists by Thomas Johnson of the King's Bath in 1675. It is 'like a seething pot', occupied at the centre by an elaborate spired conduit, around which men and women disport themselves in various stages of undress. A crowd of onlookers, and a background of Elizabethan and Jacobean houses, gabled, balustraded and heavily casemented, heighten the atmosphere of intense, grubby vitality. It could almost be Shakespeare's London, and the conduct of the populace was not refined. In an age of improvements, John Wood the elder claimed that during Charles I's time 'the streets and publick ways of the city were become like so many dunghills, slaughter-houses, and pig-styes . . . The baths were like so many bear gardens, and modesty was entirely shut out of them; people of both sexes bathing by day and night naked; and dogs, cats, pigs, and even human creatures were hurl'd over the rails into the water . . .'.

Balancing this squalor was the reputation the waters had acquired for fertility and healing, which was enhanced by royal visits. There is a story that on one occasion Anne of Denmark, wife of James I, witnessed a remarkable instance of spontaneous combustion, while she was immersed in the King's Bath. A sudden flame sprang out of the water and spread over the surface. Terrified, she hastened to the New Bath, known ever since as the Queen's Bath in her honour. But it was Queen Anne of England who inaugurated Bath's new age, by making regular use of the spa. From the time of her first visit in 1702, society flocked to the town in ever increasing numbers, and as Daniel Defoe jadedly observed, 'We may now say it is the resort of the sound as well as the sick and a place that helps the indolent and gay to commit the worst of all murders – to kill time.'

Georgian spring

The new social set brought along a train of pickpockets, cardsharpers, promiscuous women, roistering men and idle landed gentry. But for the emergence of one key figure, Bath would have kept its unsavoury reputation. This was Richard 'Beau' Nash, son of a Carmarthen glassmaker, who came to Bath in 1705 after a series of interrupted careers. He was educated at Jesus College, Oxford, but left without taking a degree. Then he entered the army, and almost immediately threw aside the commission his father had bought him, taking up the study of law instead. But that respectable occupation afforded him little delight compared with the pleasures of gaming and the love of women. For a time he lived off his wits, raising money by betting wildly, and Bath attracted him as a new arena for his activities. But he was far more than a common gambler or seducer. His personality, mingling authority, caprice, common sense and plain impudence, influenced well-bred people to an unusual degree. When the brawling, dissolute Captain Webster was killed in a duel, Nash succeeded him as Bath's official Master of Ceremonies and immediately instituted a series of reforms. These ranged from forbidding such social misdemeanours as the wearing of swords or riding boots in the ballroom to urging the Corporation to repair the roads and regulate the charges of the obstreperous sedan chairmen. He brought in an excellent orchestra from London to elevate the tone of entertainment, and formulated a famous set of civilising rules for society, faintly insolent but finely phrased – such as 'That all whisperers of lies

The chantry chapel of Prior Birde, in the south aisle of the Abbey chancel. It was begun in 1515 and has a beautifully fan-vaulted ceiling. The decoration on the wall is a carving of the prior's arms, his initials and his rebus (punning emblem), a bird.

and scandals be taken for their authors' and 'That the elder ladies and children be content with a second bench at the ballroom, as being past, or not yet come, to perfection'.

Nash became known as the king of Bath. He crowned himself with a white

The King's Bath and the Pump Room, seen from the Roman Baths.

The north side of Beaufort Square, one of Georgian Bath's earliest developments (1727), gives an impression of the unassuming scale of the town's buildings before the Woods began work. The architect was John Strahan of Bristol. He also designed Kingsmead Square and the far from unassuming Rosewell House (1736) at its west end, a baroque capriccio that looks decidedly bizarre in the context of the Woods' decorous structures.

beaver hat, so that everyone should know it. He made love to pretty visitors, yet was also protective to innocent young women, alternating between solicitude and seduction. Undeniably an attractive character, he was not handsome to look at, being big-nosed and bull-faced, but his conduct was irradiated by chivalry and quixotic bursts of generosity. He gave money out of his own pocket to hungry colliery workers marching on the town, and once handed over all his winnings at the gaming table to a low-spirited man who envied the small fortune he had amassed. 'Go, and be happy!' he urged. He never married, but kept a succession of mistresses, the last of whom was deliciously called Juliana Papjoy (commemorated in the name of the restaurant occupying Nash's last house in Sawclose), and died in poverty aged 86. The new gambling acts and a series of lawsuits had depleted his income. But the Corporation put on a suitable display of pomp for his funeral, and later Dr Harington, physician to the Bath Hospital, composed his epitaph in the Abbey:

> If social Virtues make rememb'rance dear,
>   Or Manners pure on decent rule depend;
> To His remains consign one grateful Tear,
>   Of Youth the Guardian, and of All the Friend . . .

17

Nash converted Bath from raucous to genteel behaviour, and set social standards for the whole nation. But he was not the decisive force operating in the town. The man who allied his vision with adequate economic ballast was Ralph Allen, the son of an innkeeper of St Blazey, Cornwall. He was born in 1693 and at the age of 18 he came to Bath, where he was made Assistant Postmaster. Quick promotion followed, and in 1712 he was appointed Postmaster. Alarmed to discover the dishonesty of others in his profession, he set about instituting reforms, assisted by Marshal Wade, who later became famous for laying the military roads of Scotland. (It was reputedly Allen's discovery of a Jacobite plot around Bath which first commended him to the older man.) Allen implemented a system of cross-posts for England, allaying the inconvenience of sending everything through London, and accrued enormous profits from his innovations – something in the region of £12,000 a year. He invested this wisely in the Avon Navigation Company, which made the river navigable to Bristol, and then began to develop the quarries of Combe Down.

London architects had long dismissed Bath stone as too soft for building (although the Romans had proved the contrary), and Allen was determined to restore to prominence this beautiful pale oolitic rock. So he opened the quarries, and devised a tramway line (following the course of the present Ralph Allen's Drive) operating on a system of weights and pulleys, rather like a gravity railway, to transport the stone to the Avon, where it could be conveyed by barge. He hoped to trade the stone in London, but for once he failed; it was too

Beau Nash's last house, now Popjoy's Restaurant, in Sawclose. Juliana Papjoy was Nash's last mistress, a dressmaker and herb-gatherer who lived here with him, and who never recovered from the shock of his death. The splendid entrance, further to the left and at right angles to the street, is now masked by the frontage of the Theatre Royal, attached to a building in which Nash had previously lived.

The interior of the Grand Pump Room. It measures 60 × 46 feet and is 34 feet high. In the 18th century it was sparsely furnished: after taking the waters visitors would promenade elegantly up and down, to see and be seen. From beneath the musicians' gallery, shown here, the Pump Room Trio provides accompaniment to mid-morning refreshment for present-day visitors.

porous to withstand erosion by the terrible acid smogs of the capital. But in Bath itself it enjoyed a spectacular triumph. Allen envisaged a town which utilised to best effect the lovely setting, a basin in the softly curving wooded hills. Fortunately he found an architect who was possessed of similarly boundless ambition and also had a tincture of grandiosity: John Wood.

Born in Bath in 1704, Wood worked for aristocratic patrons in London and Yorkshire before returning to his native city in 1727, seeing it as a likely place in which he could realise his architectural ideas. Certain of his writings display a surprising mystical cast. He wrote books on the megalithic monuments at Stonehenge and Stanton Drew and their significance as astronomical temples, and he maintained that each of the seven hills of Bath was formerly dedicated to a heavenly body, with an Apollonian temple in the centre of the ancient complex. He was also greatly interested in King Bladud, legendary founder of Bath, who made a pioneer attempt at aviation with wings he had forged himself. Such preoccupations suggest an energetic, versatile imagination, streaked with poetry, and tending always to seek harmony and pattern even in random arrangements of the landscape. Only a man with a dash of the dreamer in him could have conceived of a new Roman city with a 'grand Place of Assembly, to be called the Royal Forum of Bath; another Place, no less magnificent, for the Exhibition of Sports, to be called the Grand Circus; and a third Place, of equal State with either of the former, for the Practice of medicinal Exercises, to be called the Imperial Gymnasium.' There is something both childlike and appealing in such audacity. It hardly comes as a surprise to learn that with certain

of his business colleagues Wood tended to display a rather affected loftiness – he had reserves of self-esteem which made him intolerant of lesser talents.

Wood believed that the proportions of classical architecture were divinely inspired and that the presence of noble buildings could serve as a moral corrective and not merely as an imposing framework for motley human activities. Drawing on Roman and Palladian principles, he conceived of a city where houses were not set down in jumbles of isolated units but joined in graceful terraces, crescents and squares, all built of the lovely pale freestone and producing an effect that was regular, majestic and harmonious. Each individual house might be self-contained, separated by soaring columns or pilasters, and the severity of the strict symmetry was to be softened by green lawns, sweeping cornices and subtle contours. The present-day visitor sees the success of this conception. Certain Bath effects seem almost eerily beautiful: no other English city can show such a rare combination of composure of design and decorative ebullience.

Under the leadership of Wood and successive architects who imitated and developed his style – beginning with his son, John Wood the younger – a new town emerged, though his plan was never fully realised. The stately constructions for which the city is famous date from this period. Wood designed Queen Square (1726–36), the Parades (1740–3) and the Circus (1754–65), which was completed by his son – whose work, according to Walter Ison, represents 'the highest point of Palladian achievement in Bath'. The younger Wood designed the Royal Crescent (1767–75), the Upper Assembly Rooms (1768–81) and the

The garden in Queen Square, the elder Wood's first major development in Bath, with the obelisk which Nash caused to be erected in Prince Frederick's honour in 1738 (see p. 58); Wood was very proud of it. Originally it formed a more commanding centre-piece, for the garden was laid out symmetrically round it in parterres planted with flowering shrubs, enclosed by espaliered limes and elms, and bordered with gravel walks. Wood himself lived in Queen Square, on the north side, while Dr Oliver, physician to the General Hospital and inventor of the Oliver biscuit, had a house on the west side, behind the present Reference Library.

Hot Baths (now the Old Royal Baths) in Beau Street (1775–8). Thomas Baldwin created the Guildhall (1776) and the Pump Room (1789–99, completed by John Palmer), Thomas Atwood was responsible for the Paragon (1769–71), and Pulteney Bridge (1770) was designed by Robert Adam.

Bath now had its regular social 'season', like London, attended each year by all the fashionable and well-to-do. Nash's biographer, the writer Oliver Goldsmith (1730–74), describes some of its rituals. On arrival, the visitor was greeted by a peal of bells and the town musicians (he had to pay half a guinea to the ringers and half a crown to the players). Each morning began with bathing between 6 a.m. and 9 a.m., followed by a general assembly in the Pump Room for conversation, mineral water – three glasses was the recommended dose – and chamber music. An interval for coffee at different coffee houses for men and women preceded a large communal breakfast. Evenings were spent at the theatre, the gaming tables or the ball; dancing began at 6 p.m. and finished promptly at 11 p.m. The social scene was satirised by Christopher Anstey in his *New Bath Guide* (1766), an epistolary verse novel which is neither delicate (considering its author was a gentleman) nor all that funny (considering it made Horace Walpole 'bepiss' his cheeks laughing), but maintains a robust tone of swaggering jocularity:

One of the six aquatints in Thomas Rowlandson's satirical series 'The Comforts of Bath' (1798): an evening party in the Assembly Rooms.

> But who is that bombasin lady so gay,
> So profuse of her beauties in sable array;
> How she rests on her heel, how she turns out her toe,

How she pulls down her stays, with her head up to shew
Her lilywhite bosom that rivals the snow;
'Tis the widow Quicklackit, whose husband last week,
Poor Stephen, went suddenly forth in a pique,
And push'd off his boat for the Stygian creek.

The manners and attitudes of Regency Bath are memorably recorded in the novels of Jane Austen, a frequent visitor and resident who lived chiefly at Sydney Place (1801–5) and whose father is buried in Walcot churchyard. She disliked the 'glaring' whiteness of Bath stone in the sun and the mists of rain filling the valley in bad weather, and was unimpressed by the level of entertainment. But nineteen chapters of *Northanger Abbey* and nine of *Persuasion* are set in Bath, a social milieu in which everyone is dislocated from their normal setting and pretension and deceit, wittily exposed by the author, ensnare the unwary. Her precise location of scenes brings the city to life and gives us the exact flavour of the various parts of the town ('"Westgate Buildings must have been rather surprised by the appearance of a carriage drawn near its pavement", observed Sir Walter').

Victorian industry

The aura of sophistication evoked by Bath need not blind the visitor to the fact that behind the noble frontages are the pipes and drains of any working city, and Bath has always had its industries as well as its life of pleasure. Chaucer's 'Wife of Bath' was highly skilled at the loom as well as at husband-trapping. Cloth was the basis of the medieval settlement's economy, and the industry flourished during the Georgian and Regency periods, when suburbs like Walcot and Twerton housed hundreds of men and women employed in making yarn. The Kennet and Avon Canal (completed 1810) took coal and agricultural produce to London. Tourism was also important, then as now; the crowds of visitors needed their appetites assuaged, and in 1831 Bath employed one third of all the pastrycooks in Somerset.

Since medieval times there had been a market centring on the Guildhall, which transformed the area into a kind of grubby Arabian bazaar until the municipal reforms of 1851. Stalls were set up along the road: items like Staffordshire ware cluttered the paved ways together with fruit and vegetables and piles of fish. The vendors sometimes lit fires in cold weather and there was a continuous line of them stretching from Upper Borough Walls to Cheap Street. They conveyed their goods on light barrows drawn by pairs of lurcher dogs, and illuminated their wares with naphtha flares at night. Street characters abounded, creating their own folklore. During the 1890s the sober tone of social life was relieved by men like Guinea Pig Jack, with his performing rodents; Billy Madoo, a perpetually hopeful and perpetually disappointed candidate for local council elections; Farmer One-Cow, who grazed his solitary beast on the grass verge at Lansdown; and Punch Newton, a police sergeant who stubbornly refused to arrest anyone.

After a decline in Bath's fortunes as a fashionable resort during the Regency period, the spa became popular again towards the end of the 19th century. Meanwhile a new industrial age was ushered in along the banks of the Avon and in the outer suburbs. Engineering, printing and brassmaking concerns ex-

panded. In the Camden Works Museum (Julian Road, off Lansdown Road) one such business, the works of a local brass founder, engineer and mineral water manufacturer, has been restored, and the visitor can see what the operation of a 19th-century family firm was like. Isambard Kingdom Brunel designed the first railway station – an essay in the Tudor picturesque – for the Great Western Railway in 1840, and other lines followed, the Midland Region in 1870 and the 'Slow and Dirty' (Somerset and Dorset) in 1874.

The modern city

During the 20th century light industry continued to develop, and the town became noted for such products as reproduction furniture, giant building cranes, invalid carriages, corsets, plasticine and tennis balls. It is also famous, of course, for Dr Oliver's biscuits, or 'Bath Olivers', which are still manufactured, though no longer made in Bath. In 1925 the Bath Act was passed, ruling that new buildings must be faced with a substance resembling Bath stone. The

OVERLEAF
The city from Widcombe Hill.

23

freestone itself had become too expensive to work, so a substitute was developed, based on crushed limestone.

The city's long cultural tradition was consolidated in 1947 with the founding of the yearly music festival, which brings together performers of the first rank from all over the world; distinguished past directors include Yehudi Menuhin and Michael Tippett. In 1965 another foundation stone in the city's history was laid with the creation of Bath University on Claverton Down, an institution noted for its technological emphasis. The Minsistry of Defence, which established its headquarters in Bath during World War II, has become a permanent fixture.

Early morning in the market, which adjoins the Guildhall. The right to hold a market in the High Street area was granted by royal charter in medieval times, and it has been held here ever since.

A welcome modern venture is the reopening of the Kennet and Avon Canal. Trips can be taken on it in diesel hydraulic paddle vessels, which chug past former smithies, malthouses, loading bays and weighing stations. Elegant fretwork bridges made of cast iron, painted sugary white, span the waters, the work of Stothert and Pitt, a Bath firm now famous for its gigantic cranes.

Besides modern endowments which have enhanced the town, there have been grave losses, such as the demolition of hundreds of Georgian artisans' houses, and their replacement with brutal structures of plateglass and artificial stone. Conversely, many of the major architectural ensembles and individual buildings have remained unaltered and indeed have been improved by cleaning (with water, any other method being too drastic). Recent decades have seen a renewal of the city's attractions as an elegant resort, graced with museums, art galleries, excellent restaurants, and a wealth of shops selling antiques, books, clothes and food of every kind. In the unbroken tradition of centuries, Bath continues to delight its many visitors and its fortunate residents with a full and varied programme of entertainment in an unparalleled setting.

The Beauty of Bath

In and around the centre

The Abbey Church Yard is the focal point of Bath, with the Abbey to the east and the Baths and Pump Room to the south; and this view of the Great Bath and Abbey juxtaposes the city's Roman and medieval aspects. It must have been an exciting day in 1755 when workmen, demolishing the old Abbey House or Priory, came across Saxon coffins, and hot springs beneath the rubble. After that, little was done until 1878, when the City Engineer, Major Davis, proceeded with a series of excavations laying bare the Great Bath – an awesome Roman edifice measuring 83×40 feet, with lead-sheeted floors and broad steps leading down to the water. The original timber roof (which the steam probably rotted) was replaced in the late 2nd or early 3rd century by a higher concrete vault supported on massive arched columns, lit by windows at the top and open at both ends to allow the steam to escape. After the Roman legions were withdrawn from Britain, repairs were no longer made and the columns and vault collapsed into a mire of mud and vegetation. The marsh birds recolonised their former habitat and rushes began to spread. Amid all the excavated imperial impedimenta, one of the more touching items was a perfectly preserved teal's egg. Later the Saxons used the area above the baths as a burial ground – hence the coffins. The Victorians added their improvisations to the ensemble, a balustraded terrace running above the Great Bath adorned with statues of Roman emperors and governors.

According to Celtic legend, Bladud, eldest son of King Lud, lived in the 8th century BC and was intelligent, handsome and charming. But when the white spot of leprosy appeared on his hand, he had to be sent away, and for a while he lived rough, eating berries and hiding in the dense oak woods. Eventually he found employment of an unambitious sort, as a swineherd at Swainswick (some sources say Swineford), and pursued the profession ably until he noticed, to his horror, that sores were appearing on the pigs. But one day soon after, the animals, on seeing a cornucopia of acorns by the River Avon, plunged into a warm, muddy swamp there and started snorting ecstatically. When they emerged, their skins had begun to heal. Bladud tried the experiment on himself and was cured. So he was able to return to the court of his parents, where he was received with great joy. In later years he built a palace above the hot swamp and became a master of mathematics, philosophy and druidical magic. But he was by disposition an overreacher, intent on entering the domain of the gods. He managed to create a pair of workable wings, but a mechanical failure in mid-flight caused him to plunge to his death. He was succeeded by his son Lear, who was to experience an even more tragic life. The robed statue of Bladud is set in a niche in the wall of the King's Bath and can be seen from the Pump Room. It bears the inscription: 'BLADUD SON OF LUDHUDIBRAS / EIGHTH KING OF THE BRITANS / FROM BRUTE A GREAT PHILOSOPHER / & MATHEMATICIAN, BRED AT / ATHENS & RECORDED THE FIRST / DISCOVERER AND FOUNDER OF / THESE BATHS, EIGHT HUNDRED / SIXTY THREE YEARS BEFORE / CHRIST, THAT IS TWO THOUSAND / FIVE HUNDRED SIXTY TWO YEARS / TO THE PRESENT YEAR 1696.'

Right: The Great Bath and the south-west angle of the Abbey.

The great complex of baths can claim to be the finest Roman survival of its kind north of the Alps and one of the most impressive Roman monuments in Britain. It has been likened to a modern-day sports centre, not a very ennobling comparison, but containing more than a grain of truth, for facilities extended beyond simple bathing. Under the elegant colonnades were spaces in which to play games or take exercise, stalls selling wine and honey cakes, and benches for sitting, dicing, and discussing intrigues with native women or the latest news from Gaul. Here off-duty troops, officers and officials came to be immersed in steam and warm water, to be oiled, sanded, and scraped clean with a bronze strigil, to be massaged and pummelled and finally to take the cold plunge in the frigidarium. Our pictures show part of the hypocaust – the underfloor hot-air system – and the circular cold plunge bath (early 2nd century).

From the Roman Baths the visitor can

look through an arch to the King's Bath, which can also be seen from the windows of the Pump Room (see p. 16). Here during the 17th century Pepys and many others cavorted in promiscuous nakedness, men and women together – provoking numerous strictures from self-appointed guardians of public morality. The King's Bath stands over the great reservoir of the springs, and the water, rising from a shaft, once flowed over a stone basin in the centre. Around the sides ran ornamental balustrading, some of it still standing, erected in the 17th century at the expense

Left: Part of the hypocaust in the Roman Baths. Above: The cold plunge bath.

of Sir Francis Stonor of Oxfordshire, in gratitude for the baths' successful cure of his chronic gout (he lived to be 90). The old Queen's Bath, built in 1576 to provide for the increasing number of bathers, formerly adjoined the King's Bath, but was removed during the excavations of 1885–6. It took its name from Anne of Denmark, queen of James I, who bathed in it in 1616.

In 1704 Bath's distinguished physician Dr William Oliver published his treatise on the benefits of bathing in and drinking the waters, and in 1705 Bath Corporation appointed John Harvey to design a Pump Room for visitors. His one-storey building was erected the next year, and seems to have been a graceful, serviceable structure; but as the popularity of the spa increased, it was thought that something grander was needed. In 1784 the City Architect, Thomas Baldwin, added an annexe with water closets, and two years later he put up the handsome colonnade of unfluted Ionic columns. He designed the pediments above them to be carved with female sphinxes and the Aesculapian serpent on either side of an oval wreath containing the head of Hygeia – a solemn invocation of Grecian deities that attracted some civilised mockery at the time. The foundation stone of the Grand Pump Room was laid in 1788; designed initially by Baldwin, the new building was later added to by John Palmer. The north front can be glimpsed through the colonnade, fronted with an attached portico of soaring Corinthian columns, with five oval windows oddly set between them. In commemoration of the hot springs' first recorded cure (see p. 28), a wreath of oak leaves and acorns adorns the pediment. The frieze of the entablature declares in Greek that 'Water is best' (Pindar), and it was here that the social élite came to see and be seen and partake of the curious liquid which tasted (according to Dickens' Sam Weller) 'like warm flat irons'. The interior gives a pleasant lift to the spirits, with its gilding, cream paint and crystal, and there is fine reproduction Hepplewhite and Chippendale furniture to sit on while taking tea and listening to the Pump Room trio (see p. 19).

After his plans had been accepted by Parliament under the Bath Improvement Act (1789), Baldwin went on to design the delightful colonnaded walkway of Bath Street, which joins the baths in Stall Street with the Cross Bath. This bath's name is of great antiquity: it can be traced back to 1302, when a lease of the Dean and Chapter of Wells refers to 'a house in the corner as you go to the bath of the cross'. Evidently there was an ancient cross sited on the spring, which prompted John Wood the elder to speculate that 'the cross . . . was set up for a token of converting the hot waters from the patronage of the Sun to that of Christ'. The 16th-century historian John Leland found the bath 'temperate and pleasant', with 'eleven or twelve arches of stone in the sides for men to stonde under yn tyme of reyne', and 'much frequentid of people deseasid with lepre, pokkes, scabbes and great aches'.

Left: The north front of the Pump Room in the Abbey Church Yard.

In the Grand Pump Room (left) the bull-faced Beau Nash, reformer of Bath's social life, presides over the scene, his hand resting on the plan of the General Hospital, which he was instrumental in creating. (The statue is by Prince Hoare, and was done in the mid 1750s.) The long-case clock was made by the great English maker Thomas Tompion, who presented it to the city in 1709 together with a sun-dial to check its accuracy. (Above) The dome of the Concert Room, an extension to the Pump Room added by John Brydon in 1897; Charles Robertson described it as 'a handsome room, and the best Victorian interior in Bath'.

Bath Abbey, seen here from the south-west, sailing above the parapet of the Roman Baths, stands challenging and authoritative at the core of the city. The existing building, on the site of the nave of the Norman cathedral, is essentially Perpendicular Gothic, and was begun in 1499. Its plan is a simple cross shape, but the serrated parapet of pierced arcading and the elaborate fenestration make it appear fragile and jewel-like – an effect counterbalanced by the big square tower and powerful flying buttresses. The 52 windows have led it to be described as 'the lantern of England'. Sir George Gilbert Scott's extensive restorations (1859–74) were faithful to the original designers' probable intentions, and included renewal of the attractive openwork pinnacles. The turrets on the west front are embellished with 16th-century sculptures of the dream ladder seen by Bishop King (see above, p. 10). The angels ascend the rungs to the Trinity at the top in a rather awkward, monkeyish fashion, and some look as if they are impaled like moths to the stone;

as one observer has pointed out, it is a formidable artistic problem to depict figures expressing divinity and grace while climbing a ladder.

Inside, one's first impressions are of the towering east and west windows and the fan-vaulted roof. Unlike most other English cathedrals and abbeys, Bath has an uninterrupted view from west to east, because there is no screen and the altar is against the east wall, and this makes the visitor feel very quickly at home. The master craftsmen chosen by Prior Birde to build the Abbey were Robert and William Vertue, the king's masons, who also worked on Henry VII's chapel in Westminster Abbey and St George's Chapel, Windsor.

They planned to use fan-vaulting – at that date virtually unknown in England; but their work was left incomplete until later phases of building, and the vaulting we see now dates from the late 16th century (the crossing), the 17th century (the south transept) and the 19th century (the nave).

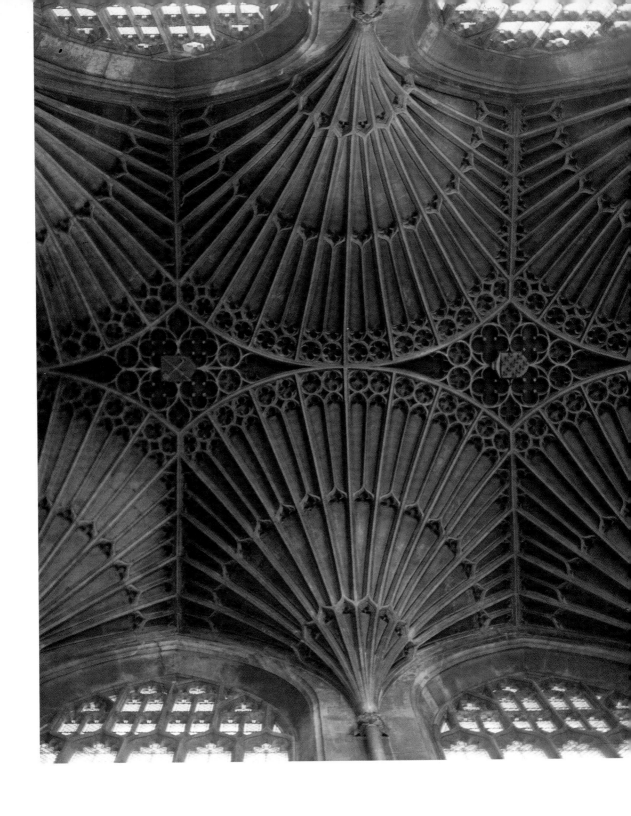

Left: The Abbey from the south-west. Above: Fan-vaulting in the Abbey.

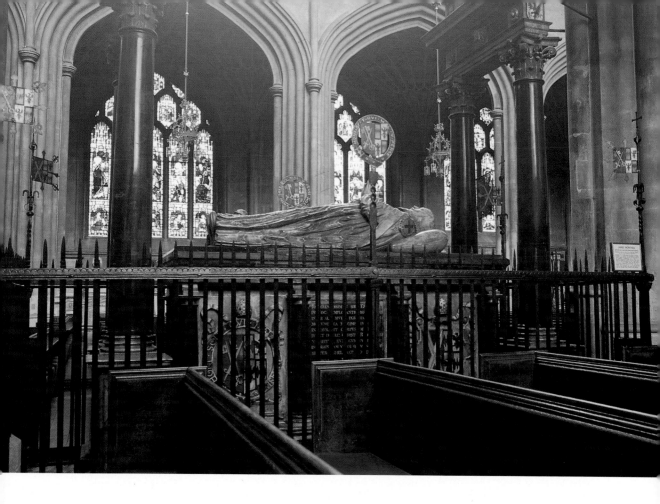

After the Dissolution of the monasteries in 1539, the condition of the Abbey rapidly worsened, and merchants bought all the glass, bells, iron and lead; the latter alone, Sir John Harington calculated, amounted to 480 tons and was worth £4800. Queen Elizabeth initiated its restoration, and it was Harington (her godson) who persuaded Bishop Montague to complete the work. A story recounts how the two dignitaries were walking through Bath one day when a rainstorm drove them inside the Abbey. Leadless and leaking, it afforded them scant shelter. As the rain soaked them through, Sir John pointedly remarked, 'How, if the church does not save us from water above, can it save us from fire below?' Montague proved a liberal benefactor, and though he later became bishop of Winchester, he retained his attachment to Bath and directed that he should be buried here. Above his splendid tomb in the north aisle (1618), designed by William Cuer and carved by Nicholas Johnson, rise black Corinthian columns crowned with griffins, shields, and coats of arms; the alabaster bishop lies praying, in full, flowing robes, his back supported by a cushion.

The Abbey is especially rich in memorials, of varying artistic and literary expressiveness, and it is well worth taking a walk round to look at them; many of the inscriptions vividly evoke the attitudes and manners of 18th-century society, and much of the sculpture is rewardingly inventive. In the south chancel aisle a tablet by Flaxman dated 1796 commemorates Dr John Sibthorp, author of the *Flora Graeca*, in suitably Greek style – the hat and cloak he wears and the ship he is stepping into are all reminiscent of ancient Greek monuments to those who died at sea (as he did); and in his hand he carries, appropriately, a bunch of herbs. Equally compelling is the beautifully carved memorial to Jacob Bosanquet (died 1767) by W.C. Carter, in the south transept, which shows the Good Samaritan, with his lively horse tethered to a tree, and the priest and the Levite keeping their distance.

At the east end of the north chancel aisle is a modern window (1949) depicting one of the greatest moments in the Abbey's history, the coronation of King Edgar in 973. St Dunstan, Archbishop of Canterbury, is about to place the crown on the king's head, while he holds the orb and sceptre in his hands.

Memorials in the Abbey. Left: Bishop Montague's tomb. Below: The wall tablet of the Good Samaritan commemorating Jacob Bosanquet.

The present Guildhall was built between 1766 and 1778 to a design by Thomas Baldwin; he was still only 27 when it was finished. It replaced a building erected in 1625, which, according to the not invariably reliable John Wood the elder, owed something to Inigo Jones, who had drafted a design 'from a natural inclination to render the city all the service in his power, his mother being a native of Bath, and daughter of one of the chief master-clothiers in the city'. Baldwin's Guildhall is massively impressive, with ground-floor rusticated arches, lofty Ionic columns, and a pediment supporting a statue of Justice (without the usual blindfold). The dome and the cupola-crowned extensions on either side were later additions (1891) by John Brydon, who also did the additions to the Pump Room.

Inside is the splendid Banqueting Room, according to Ison 'beyond any question the finest interior in Bath'. All its elements contribute to an air of elegant festivity: the proportions (80 × 40 × 31 feet), the arched recesses between painted Corinthian columns around the walls, the frieze of neoclassical motifs – garlands and gilded rams' heads – the four-tier crystal chandeliers, and the delicate plasterwork ceiling panels.

The Guildhall enjoyed a period of celebrity, but had become rather less fashionable by Victoria's reign, as the comment of Angelo Cyrus Bantam in Dickens' *Pickwick Papers* (1836) suggests: 'The ball-nights in Ba-ath are moments snatched from Paradise, rendered bewitching by music, beauty, elegance, fashion, etiquette, and – and – above all, by the absence of tradespeople, who are quite inconsistent with Paradise and have an amalgamation of themselves at the Guildhall every fortnight.'

The Guildhall. Left: The High Street front. Above: The Banqueting Room.

41

Northumberland Place is a beguiling alley between Union Passage and the High Street, flower-hung in summer and lined with cafés and small businesses. This is the heart of the pedestrianised area, where shoppers push and bustle: anything can be got here, from brassware to jodhpurs, from antiquarian books to delicatessen food. Although it was built on land owned by the Duke of Northumberland, the terminal arch bears the coat of arms of Frederick Augustus, Duke of York and Albany (1763–1827), second son of George III, who visited Bath in 1795 to attend the opening of the new Pump Room. The lion and unicorn, shields and a knightly helm add distinction to the pediment, but their positioning remains an enigma.

Parallel to Northumberland Place runs the Corridor, a covered arcade embellished with garlands, lions' heads, a pair of statues and a musicians' gallery. The pioneer of ciné photography William Friese-Greene had a studio at no. 7 in the 1870s.

Parade Gardens, to the east of the Abbey, makes a pleasant place to rest from the fatigues of shopping or sightseeing and listen to the band playing in the ornamental bandstand. From here there are beautiful views of the surrounding hills. Bathonians are proud of their city's regular success in the annual 'Britain in Bloom' competition, and the Parks Department puts on a special floral display in Parade Gardens each July.

Orange Grove, between Parade Gardens and the Abbey, was so named in honour of William of Orange's visit in 1734, which the obelisk in the middle commemorates (see p. 13).

Left: Northumberland Place. Above: Parade Gardens.

The end pavilions of Pulteney Bridge were originally toll houses intended to raise money for a new estate conceived by William Johnstone, a Scot who had married the heiress Frances Pulteney. He assumed the arms and name of the aristocratic family he had joined, and on the death of his brother became the 5th Baronet of Westerhall, County Dumfries. He planned the new estate, to be called Bathwick, to grow up on the other bank of the Avon, where cattle peacefully grazed. But first he needed a new bridge to span the river, and he employed his friend and fellow Scot, Robert Adam, to draw up plans not only of the bridge but of the projected estate.

The Corporation rejected Adam's initial design, stating that it would impede circulation of the air 'and the SMOAK will greatly incommode the neighbourhood'. His Bathwick plan was never carried out, but after delays and difficulties the lovely bridge – possibly an adroit variation of Palladio's unrealised design for the Ponte di Rialto in Venice – was completed in 1774, the only Adam building in Bath. There is no other bridge in England like it: triple-arched, high-walled, set above a sparkling weir, it has elegant walkways lined with shops selling items as varied as crusty bread, bone china, confectionery, stamps and doorknockers.

Pulteney Bridge leads across the river into Argyle Street, and then through Laura Place into the grandiose Great Pulteney Street. Adam's designs for this part of the Bathwick estate were finally rejected by Pulteney's daughter, Henrietta Laura, who had inherited the property. She chose instead to employ the local City Architect, Thomas Baldwin. Octagonal

Laura Place was designed to link up the four streets of irregular width that converged there.

The awesome thoroughfare of Great Pulteney Street has been used as a starting point for motor rallies (architectural Wagnerianism has its peculiar disadvantages), being 100 feet wide and 1100 feet long. Corinthian pilasters, pediments, and rusticated ground floors – the pattern is familiar enough though the scale is out of proportion with a city of Bath's size, and a few houses retain lampholders and original ironwork to enhance their appeal. Closing the view is the Holburne of Menstrie Museum, built as the Sydney Hotel in 1796. This splendid collection, based on one made by Sir Thomas William Holburne in the early 19th century, includes some of the best 17th- and 18th-century

Pulteney Bridge. Left: From the river. Above: Shops on the Bridge, with part of the Guildhall on the right.

silver in Britain, Roman glass, cameos, seals and coins, and miniatures, ceramics and porcelain. There are paintings by Gainsborough, Guardi, Stubbs, Turner and Zoffany among others.

In 1850 a fountain craze swept Bath, and produced a 'General Committee for Promoting the Erection of Public Fountains in this City'. It was decided to set up an exemplar in Laura Place, and this was duly completed in 1877. (The present fountain is modern.) The dream of the Georgian city being further enhanced by gushing liquid spires never came true – there simply wasn't enough tappable water.

Bath has had innumerable famous residents, and Great Pulteney Street in particular, a fashionable address during the 18th and 19th centuries, is rich in commemorative plaques. Lord Macaulay, the writer and statesman, stayed at no. 1. In 1867 and 1872 Lord Lytton (Bulwer Lytton), author of *The Last Days of Pompeii*, stayed at no. 2. No. 6 was the home of the City Architect and designer of the street, Thomas Baldwin. William Smith (1769–1839), known as 'the father of English geology', and also as Strata Smith, because he established the identification of rock strata by their fossil population, lived at no. 29. The great reformer William Wilberforce (1759–1833), who devoted his career to the abolition of slavery, stayed at no. 36 in 1802 and 1805. Prince Louis Napoleon, later Napoleon III, stayed at no. 55. Earl Howe (Admiral Howe), who achieved distinction in the War of the Austrian Succession, the Seven Years War and as victor of the 'glorious 1st of June' in the Channel during the French Revolutionary Wars, stayed at no. 71 in 1794, 1795 and 1798. No. 76, one of the first houses to be put up, was built for Hannah More, who lived there with her sister from 1792 to 1802. A woman of great energy and evangelising zeal, she opened schools and Sunday schools in the Mendip region and brought religion and education to country children. She tended to describe rather too many rustic communities as 'savage' or 'depraved', and Dr Johnson characteristically called her 'the old bishop in petticoats', but she was well-meaning and impressive.

Below: Houses in Bathwick Hill. Right: An aerial view of Great Pulteney Street towards the Holburne of Menstrie Museum. The Abbey can be seen in the foreground.

Lilliput Alley, with its Swiftian echoes, was renamed North Parade Passage in the later 18th century. Its oldest building is Sally Lunn's House, said to have been erected in the late 15th century, but now with a 17th-century façade and sash windows. The name comes from a woman who sold cakes from the premises around 1680, and this tradition continues – Sally Lunn's is a noted teashop. The basement contains the original ovens. Etymologists have derived the name from *sol et lune*, a celestial interpretation encouraged by the lack of any historical record of Sally Lunn.

Lilliput Alley was also the site of the town house of one of Bath's greatest citizens, Ralph Allen (see p. 18); the magnificent Palladian garden front (1727) can be glimpsed between later encroachments from York Street, round the corner. In 1762 Allen decided to improve the view by adding a sham castle to the distant hillside: the Gothick façade, complete with arrow slits and castellated towers, can be seen to the east from York Street. It may be by Sanderson Miller, the celebrated architect of eyecatchers.

Abbey Green is a memorial to the monastic establishment of Bath, which came to an end in 1539. At the Dissolution the monks' domestic buildings, orchards and plots of land were dispersed into private hands. A tiny relic remains in the form of a hinge set into the wall of St Michael's Arch (named after the patron saint of adjoining Marks and Spencer's), which opens on to Abbey Green. Nos. 2 and 2a have been restored by the Bath Preservation Trust and are now shops.

Left: Sally Lunn's House. Below: Abbey Green.

Abbey Church House, built for Edward Clarke in 1570 and restored after bombing in 1942, is virtually the single remnant of Elizabethan Bath. Called successively Hungerford House when the Hungerfords of Farleigh Castle acquired it, Lexington House when it was owned by Lord Lexington (who married a Hungerford), Savill's Lodgings until about 1714, Skrine's Lower House (Skrine was a chemist, who married Mrs Savill), and Hetling House after William Hetling, a wealthy tradesman, it was renamed Abbey Church House in 1888, when the rector and churchwardens of the Abbey bought it. The Great Room, upstairs, has a fine Tudor chimneypiece. A pump room was built at the back, to which Jane Austen's brother Edward resorted in 1799. He sampled the water internally and externally, underwent electrical treatment, and lived to be 84 – despite his sister's scepticism about such remedies.

A passage on the north-west side of the house called Hetling Court leads to Chapel Court, a peaceful backwater reminiscent of a small college courtyard at Oxford or Cambridge. Here stands St John's Hospital, founded in 1180 by Bishop Reginald for poor sick townspeople. Later its occupants wore blue gowns and became known as the 'Blue Alms'. In the 1720s the Duke of Chandos, who had stayed in lodgings above the almshouses and found them less than luxurious, decided to rebuild the whole layout as a close, complete with a town house for himself, new almshouses, and lodgings for visitors to the Cross Bath nearby. The hospital was restored in 1877–8, when new wings were added.

St James's Parade, south of Abbey Church House, was originally a quiet cul-de-sac. The south-east side is especially attractive, with Venetian windows, pedimented doorways and prominent cornices.

Right: Abbey Church House. Below: St James's Parade.

The foundation stone of the new Theatre Royal was laid in 1804; George Dance the younger was the principal architect. It is his only building in Bath, and the 'Gallic fastidiousness' of his detail has been praised by Walter Ison. The restored Grand Front to Beaufort Square is the most impressive side, though the ground floor has been altered since Dance's day. Light, unemphatic pilasters rise between the bays to a frieze carved with players' masks, recalling early Greek drama, and a ribboned garland. The small parapet above is tricked out with stone lyres and an almost boastfully eyecatching Royal Arms. Nowadays the theatre is run by a charitable trust, and presents a wide variety of programmes. The previous Theatre Royal was the one in Orchard Street – now the Freemasons' Hall –

opened in 1750 by John Palmer and his son. The younger Palmer's frequent communication with London in search of actors inspired his invention of the mail coach, which revolutionised the speed and efficiency of the country's postal system. Bath has a prominent place in postal history; the Postal Museum is at 8 Broad Street.

In the Abbey is a memorial by one of England's greatest actors to another – verses composed by Garrick in memory of Quin, who died in Bath in 1766, aged 73. The friend of Pope and Swift, and the supreme Falstaff of his age, he also gave elocution lessons to the infant George III.

Above: The Theatre Royal. Right: James Quin's memorial in the Abbey.

OB: MDCCLXVI
ÆTAT: LXXIII

That tongue *which set the table on a roar,*
And charm'd the public ear, is heard no more:
Clos'd are thofe eyes, the harbingers of wit,
Which fpake before the tongue what *SHAKESPEAR* writ:
Cold is that hand, which living was ftretch'd forth,
At friendfhip's call, to fuccour modeft worth:
Here lies JAMES QUIN: deign, reader, to be taught,
Whate'er thy ftrength of body, force of thought,
In nature's happieft mould however caft,
To this complexion thou muft come at laft.

D: GARRICK

The out-of-the-way no. 5 Trim Street is known as Wolfe's House, after General Wolfe (1727–59), a gifted soldier who was born and brought up in Westerham, Kent. After taking part in various campaigns, including the War of the Austrian Succession and the pacification of the Scottish Highlands, he was sent to North America and put in charge of the attack on Quebec. He effectively lured the French out of the city and routed them, but died of a musket wound on the Heights of Abraham. A famous painting by Benjamin West (National Gallery of Canada) depicts the dying hero.

Wolfe was not cast in the heroic mould, being small, sandy-haired, almost chinless and subject to regular bouts of gloom and depression. He came to Bath in 1757 when his health had deteriorated, and met and was attracted to a Miss Lowther, daughter of Robert Lowther, a former Governor of Barbados. But Wolfe was a single-minded soldier, more expert with armies than amours, and the affair never came to anything. It is said that it was during his stay in Bath that he heard he was to lead the Canadian expedition. The house, once the residence of Wolfe's parents (Trim Street was put up in 1707), is a scaled-down

version of Palladian design, possibly the work of Thomas Greenway. The martial trophies on the tympanum were added later, presumably as a compliment to the general.

Trim Street was named after George Trim, a wealthy clothier. He was a noted figure in Bath, principally because of his far-sighted expansionism. His mother was reputedly a close relation of Inigo Jones. The street has several other distinctive houses, such as no. 17 (with a shell-hood

Left: Wolfe's House, Trim Street. Above: Queen Street and Trim Bridge.

doorway), and a pretty arch at one end, over Queen Street. This is known as Trim Bridge or St John's Gate, the latter name recalling the nearby presence in former times of the city walls and ditch – Trim was one of the first speculators to disregard the Corporation's veto on building beyond the city boundaries.

Pedestrianised Old Bond Street lies at the bottom of Milsom Street. This was the commercial core of fashionable Bath in Jane Austen's day, where Isabella Thorpe of *Northanger Abbey* saw 'the prettiest little hat you can imagine in a shop window', where Sir Walter Elliot of *Persuasion* 'counted eighty-seven women go by, without there being a tolerable face among them', and where Anne Elliot and Captain Wentworth have their 'overpowering' encounter in Mrs Molland's confectionery shop.

Daniel Milsom was a wine cooper who turned to property development. In 1755 he was granted a lease by the Corporation on the land called Town Acre, north of George Street. Later, in June 1762, the *Bath Chronicle* carried an announcement that there was 'to be lett on a Building Lease for 99 years . . . a piece of Ground, lately known by the name of Milsom's Ground, situate in the parish of St Michael's'. These plots became the shopping area where James Jolly, in 1831, established an emporium selling linen, silk mercery, shawls, merinos, lace nets and a range of china and knick-knacks. His shop-front, marked with the date 1879, dominates the west side of Milsom Street. Across the road Thomas Baldwin's Somersetshire Buildings of 1782 (illustrated here in an aquatint of 1788 by Thomas Malton) still dominate their side of the street, showily stepping out of line in front and above as if the City Architect was asserting his status.

They must have seemed even more incongruous when they were built, but now, like Jolly's, they add a nice note of opulence to this invariably exhilarating thoroughfare.

Further down on the east side, it is well worth looking into the Octagon, originally a chapel (1767), now an exhibition room for the Royal Photographic Society. The design, by Thomas Lightholer, includes galleries upheld by Ionic pillars and an attractive central dome and cupola. As a chapel it was immensely fashionable, and when the vivacious Mrs Piozzi visited it to hear the Bishop of Gloucester preach, 'You will rejoice to hear,' she wrote to a friend, 'that I came out alive from . . . a crowd such as in my long life I have never witnessed: we were packed like seeds in a sunflower'. Its popularity was enhanced by the reputation of its organist, the astronomer William Herschel, who accepted the 'agreeable and lucrative situation' as a Hanoverian refugee from the French invasion. But such was his passion for optics, that upon completing his musical duties he would rush home and, without even pausing to take off his lace ruffles, would begin grinding specula and polishing lenses. He moved into King Street in 1780, and it was there, on 13 March 1781, that he discovered the planet Uranus.

Left: Somersetshire Buildings, Milsom Street, in Jane Austen's day. Below: Looking up Old Bond Street towards Milsom Street.

From Queen Square to the Royal Crescent

Queen Square was John Wood the elder's first major undertaking in Bath; building began in December 1728. The dimensions of the square are 316 feet from north to south and 306 feet from east to west. The sides differ, the north front being the showpiece: seven large houses form a powerful symmetrical composition varied by threequarter pilasters and columns, an attic storey and a lofty central pediment. The effect is almost crushingly grand, rather than domestic. The garden in the centre, originally formal, but now more as nature intended, contains an obelisk, which – at Wood's insistence – was given a tapered top. It was put up by Beau Nash in 1738 'in memory of honours conferr'd and in gratitude for benefits bestow'd in this city by his royal highness Frederick, Prince of Wales, and his royal consort', and was renovated in 1978, to commemorate the 25th anniversary of the reign of Queen Elizabeth II and the 250th anniversary of Wood's design. It is good to know that at least Nash esteemed Frederick, for his parents detested him, and his mother, the amiable Queen Caroline, said, 'My dear first-born is the greatest ass and the greatest liar and the greatest *canaille* and the greatest beast in the whole world, and I heartily wish he were out of it.'

Gay Street ascends steeply from Queen Square to the upper part of the town – the area of the great Georgian developments. Horace Walpole, who lodged in St John's Hospital in the lower town in 1766, complained that 'one cannot stir without clambering' in Bath, and 'mountains run against one's nose'.

Below: The north side of Queen Square. Right: Gay Street.

The earliest Assembly Rooms were put up in 1708 on the east side of the Terrace Walk, beside formal gardens that skirted the Avon. They were built for Thomas Harrison, who later added a ballroom with a stucco ceiling. The annual *Bath Guide* noted: 'The view of the river, valley, and adjacent hills, makes it one of the pleasantest morning rooms in the kingdom . . . elegantly furnished with chandeliers, girandoles, etc.' Another set of rooms in the lower town, Lindsey's (later Wiltshire's), was erected to a design by John Wood the elder in 1727. Neither now remains, and both were eclipsed by the creation of the Upper Assembly Rooms in Bennett Street, built in 1771 to cater for the increasing numbers of fashionable visitors to the spa. Robert Adam was

invited to submit plans, but they were rejected as too costly, and the younger Wood's less elaborate design was preferred. The Upper Rooms consisted initially of a ballroom, a tea room and a card room; they cost £20,000 to erect. The tea room was used for concerts, and here Franz Liszt and Johann Strauss the elder gave performances, and Dickens did one of his grippingly histrionic readings. The Rooms were much resorted to in order to relieve, or vary, the progress of 'routs' – private evening parties that were a pronounced feature of Regency Bath. In a letter of 1801 (by which time Bath was already slightly in decline as a fashionable venue), Jane Austen wrote that 'the breaking up of parties sent some more scores to the Ball, and tho' it was shockingly and inhumanly thin for this place, there were people enough to have made five or six very pretty Basingstoke assemblies'. The Rooms were badly damaged by bombing during World War II, but have since been faithfully restored to their original splendour. At the time of their first opening, the *Bath Guide* described the tea room (shown below in an aquatint of 1805 by Nattes):

'The entablature is of stucco, above which is a pedestal wrought in mosaic work, from whence rises a cove, the line of which is relieved by a swelling soffit of laurel leaves interspersed with berries, which are continued to and from, across and along the ceiling, rolling under each other and forming by their intersection the most beautiful network, embellished with garlands, laurels, palm branches, festoons and wreaths of flowers. This room is wainscotted the same as the Ball Room, has three glass chandeliers, and four marble chimney-pieces properly decorated, and is

lighted from the east and south sides by eight windows. Behind the Ionic colonnade, and under three stone arches carved with vine branches and grapes, is the bar, from whence over a side-table the waiters take the tea to the company.'

Nowadays the Rooms are run by the City Council and used for tea dances, antique fairs and receptions. In the basement is the famous Museum of Costume, which begins with a dress dating from the 1660s made of silver tissue – a great rarity – and continues with examples from all periods down to the present day, some arranged in tableaux of domestic settings of their time. The collection is kept absolutely up to date by the annual addition of the 'Dress of the Year', chosen by a leading fashion journalist from the work of the top designers.

The Assembly Rooms. Left: The entrance, off Bennett Street. Below: The tea room, by J. C. Nattes.

The immense circle of the Circus, designed by the Woods, is varied by Greek columns of all three orders superimposed on top of each other: Doric at the ground floor, Ionic in the second storey, Corinthian in the third. The frieze between the ground and first floors is carved with a succession of emblems of the arts, sciences and trades, almost without repetition. The parapet is adorned with stone acorns, whimsically placed there by the elder Wood to commemorate the Bladud legend (see p. 28), in which he firmly believed. He started the large undertaking in 1754 but died before its completion, leaving his son to see it through. The insistent regularity of the precisely patterned variations does not please every eye. Matthew Bramble, in Smollett's *Humphry Clinker* (1771), dismissed it as 'a pretty bauble: contrived for shew, and looks like Vespasian's amphitheatre [the Colosseum] turned outside in'. But the equidistant openings for the three adjoining streets provide contrasting angles and vistas which prevent the symmetry having a claustrophobic effect. The grassy island at the centre, from which arise magnificent shaggy plane trees, used to be a covered reservoir for the surrounding buildings – piped water was not available, and servants collected supplies in pails and containers. No foliage softened the general aspect: the middle was paved with cobbles, and purists maintain it still should be.

North of the Circus in Circus Place, suitably housed in the Circus mews, is the Carriage Museum. Its exhibits include an original Bath invalid chair, a carriage used by Queen Victoria, and the Royal Mail Coach which plied between Bristol, Bath and London. From the Circus Brock Street leads to the Royal Crescent.

Left: A detail of the Circus. Below: Brock Street.

North of Brock Street, between the Circus and the Royal Crescent, there is a broad paved way lined with flower tubs and shops. This is called Margaret's Buildings after Mrs Margaret Garrard, former Lady of the Manor and patroness of the living of Walcot. It is not an architectural showpiece, but a pedestrian precinct of civilised charm that has a sense of being used by the local community, with its newsagent, launderette, bookshop and wine bar.

The Royal Crescent is a breathtaking sight, displaying Bath magnificence at its most assertive and vying with the Circus for spectacular effect. An immense curve of grey and cream stone buildings, comprising 30 houses with 114 giant Ionic first-floor columns, forms a semi-ellipse beneath a continuous carved cornice. John Wood the younger began the project in 1767 and completed it in 1775. The concept was said to have been inspired by Bernini's colonnade surrounding the Piazza S. Pietro in Rome; it was the first time a crescent of houses was used in British architecture. There is a wide pavement of Penant sandstone and a roadway of granite setts between the buildings and the big open grassy space below, enhancing the impact of the scene – a favourite promenade for visitors for over two centuries. The approach from Brock Street has the added excitement of surprise, for the sweep of buildings is far greater than the views from the side streets lead one to expect. This was what Wood intended, for in his day the land to south and west was open fields, and Brock Street would have been the usual approach.

Left: Margaret's Buildings. Above: The Royal Crescent.

The Royal Crescent.

The Royal Victoria Park, with its bowling green, bandstand and tea rooms, is a delightful retreat. The Victoria Obelisk sports three stone lions of contrasting temperaments: one looks bored and soporific, another formidable, and the third quizzical. Medallions mounted on each side of the triangular monument record the main events of the queen's career. One shows the young Victoria in profile and notes her marriage to Prince Albert; the second tells of the death of 'Albert the Good' in 1861; and the third acknowledges the Empress of India's growing fame and her death in 1901. The obelisk was erected in 1837 to celebrate Princess Victoria's coming of age, and it was an inspired idea to use it later to chronicle her progress to the grave.

Victoria Park affords further views of the Royal Crescent. No. 1, at its eastern end, has been restored to its pristine condition and suitably decorated and furnished by the Bath Preservation Trust, and is open to the public. At one time the house was leased to Thomas Brock, the architect's father-in-law, who gave his name to nearby Brock Street. Sir Isaac Pitman, who lived at no. 17, came to Bath as a poor but zealous teacher, and in 1844 published *Stenographic Sound Hand*, introducing his new system of shorthand, which came to be used worldwide. No. 11 is famous for the sensational elopement from it in 1772 of the 17-year-old singer Elizabeth Linley with the playwright Richard Brinsley Sheridan. This was a tangled tale of patriarchal dominance engendering rebellion and fervid romance. Sheridan had to fight two duels for Elizabeth's sake, one at London which he won, and a second at Bath where he ended up prostrate, with his accuser, an older man, stabbing at him with a broken sword. By 1773 the clouds had cleared and Sheridan and Elizabeth were married.

Below: The Royal Crescent from Victoria Park. Right: The Victoria Obelisk.

Overleaf: The Circus and Crescents from the air.

Towards Lansdown

The Countess of Huntingdon's Chapel, in the Vineyards, was built by the zealous Selina, Countess of Huntingdon, for her particular branch ('Connexion') of the Methodist ministry in 1765. Bath was a city of gambling, dancing and a general relaxation of barriers and inhibitions, where the sexes could mingle freely – in Charles Wesley's opinion, 'the headquarters of Satan'. When John Wesley preached in Bath in 1739, Beau Nash told him 'your preaching frightens people out of their wits', but failed to budge the resolute evangelist. Horace Walpole, visiting the chapel in its early days, 'was glad to see that luxury is creeping in upon them before persecution; they have very neat mahogany for benches and brackets of the same in taste . . . with red cushions for the parson and clerk'. Wesley he describes as 'a lean, elderly man, fresh-coloured, his hair smoothly combed, but with a *soupçon* of curls at the end. Wondrous clean, but as evidently an actor as Garrick.' The chapel (now an educational centre) is marked on the Paragon side by its more interesting manse, with Gothick windows and doorways that make it unusual for Bath.

Hedgemead Park, beside the London Road, was the result of a landslip in the late 19th century which damaged a row of houses so badly that the area had to be cleared. The combination in Lansdown of steep banded rock strata interspersed with slippery clay, and the added pressure of development, occasionally forces a shift in the rock beds. One of the most alarming occurred in 1788, during the building of Camden Crescent, and compelled the speculators to abandon part of their plan for this desirable quarter of the town.

Below: Hedgemead Park. Right: The manse of the Countess of Huntingdon's Chapel.

Lansdown landmarks. Below: Camden Crescent. Right: St Stephen's church.

Camden Crescent (preceding pages), designed by John Eveleigh, is named after Charles Pratt, Marquis of Camden, judge, politician, and Recorder of Bath 1759–61. His arms appear on the tympanum of the pediment and his personal crest, the elephant, graces the keystone of each doorway. The view from here rewards the visitor who has made the steep climb up Belmont, and occasionally buzzards can be seen hanging over the valley.

St Stephen's church (1840–5), a prominent landmark in this area, was designed by a local architect, James Wilson. The remarkable tower, starting square and turning octagonal, has high-shooting pinnacles and flying buttresses. Pevsner found it 'crazy', but Bryan Little admired its 'fanciful, pagoda-like quality'.

Spectacular Lansdown Crescent (this page and overleaf), gracefully following the curves of Lansdown's south-east slopes, was the result of the coach-builder Charles Spackman turning property-developer and employing the architect John Palmer to design a terrace. Work was begun in 1789. Unlike the Royal Crescent, this crescent has a delightfully rustic aspect, which softens its grandeur: the slope below is a meadow, and – especially when sheep have been brought in to crop the grass – the combination of bucolic simplicity and classical pomp creates the true Georgian feel. At its western end Lansdown Crescent was joined to Lansdown Place with a little bridge (below) by the eccentric William Beckford, who lived there in the 1820s (see p. 82).

Below: Beckford's Bridge, Lansdown Crescent. Right: The centre of Lansdown Crescent.

Lansdown Crescent.

Somerset Place, a further crescent of houses attached to Lansdown Crescent at its west end, was designed by John Eveleigh in 1793. Another triumph of uniformity and decorum, it consists of a regular curved terrace emphasised by a continuous cornice and plat-band above the ground floor. The central feature captures the eye: a pair of houses carrying a broken pediment, which is beautifully carved and crowned with an urn. Somerset Place suffered heavy bombing during the war but was later restored, and taken over by the domestic science college which is now incorporated with Bath College of Higher Education.

At the top of Cavendish Road, on the slopes of Sion Hill, is the Doric House (1810), designed by J.M. Gandy (1771–1843), a pupil of Sir John Soane. Architecturally a much admired house, it has an odd and faintly sinister look, with its windowless wall, Doric columns, abaci and modillioned cornice supporting an attic storey of shorter superimposed columns and three windows. The house was funded by the wealthy coach-builder Charles Spackman (see p. 76) for the artist Thomas Barker, who came to Bath as a 13-year-old boy from Pontypool. Spackman befriended him and paid for him to attend an art school in Rome, where he refined his talents. On returning to Bath, he took up a highly successful career. Landscapes flowed off his busy brush, and one of his most effective anecdotes of bucolic life, *The Woodman*, sold for the enormous sum of 500 guineas. The interior of the Doric House contains his picture gallery and (behind the closed outer wall) his fresco *The Massacre of the Inhabitants of Scio by the Turks*, in its original position.

Further down the hill on the left is Cavendish Crescent (1817–30), designed by John Pinch (1769–1827) for the builder William Broom (who went bankrupt in 1825). This crescent has a special charm of its own: a distinctly late Regency design, its plain lines and understated decoration give it an unassuming domestic look, very different in tone from the grand Palladian gestures found elsewhere. The absence of pediments and window architraves focuses attention on the pretty rusticated arched entrances and the first-floor ironwork balconies (expanded at no. 9 to a veranda with a tent roof).

Left: Somerset Place. Below: Doric House.

On the outskirts

Lansdown Tower was the creation of William Beckford (1760–1844), who invested Georgian Bath with a darker kind of glamour. This flamboyant connoisseur of the arts and dilettante author – his novel *Vathek* (1784) introduced a tone of sinister flippancy anticipating Wilde and Firbank – lived surrounded by books and dogs and attended by his doting dwarf servant Perro. Son of the Lord Mayor of London and prodigiously wealthy, he was rich enough to be able to fantasise in three dimensions, creating a stupendous Gothick abbey at Fonthill. In 1822 he purchased the most western house of the centre section of Lansdown Crescent (no. 20), but such was his desire for space and seclusion that he later bought the last house of Lansdown Place West as well, and closed the gap with a neat little bridge adorned with a balustrade and metal urns and palms (see p. 76). The garden extended for a mile up Lansdown Hill, and at the top the architect Henry Edmund Goodridge completed this tower for Beckford in 1827.

Unlike the madcap Gothick fantasy of Fonthill, the tower is a restrained campanile, the one element of the bizarre occurring at the top, where a model of the Choragic Monument of Lysicrates at Athens, constructed of cast-iron columns and a cast-iron roof – and in Beckford's day painted and gilded – sits on the edifice like a classical crown. Beckford had the interior elaborately furnished with a Crimson Drawing Room, a Scarlet Drawing Room and an Etruscan Library. A statue of St Anthony of Padua occupied the first-floor room, known as the Sanctuary, and there was also a Vestibule and Annexe.

When Beckford died, his daughter the Duchess of Hamilton inherited the tower. She sold it to a publican who turned it into a beer garden, an affront which so disturbed her that she bought it back. Following the terms of the will, Beckford's tomb was shifted to a moated enclosure by the tower and his body reinterred beside his favourite dog. The tomb is of polished granite and bears his coat of arms and an inscription: 'Eternal Power, / Grant me through obvious clouds one transient gleam / Of thy bright essence in my dying hour.' The tower and garden later passed to the living of Walcot and the garden became a cemetery. Its overgrown and neglected state enhances the moody drama of the tower – which, however, has been restored and converted to form two private dwellings and a Beckford Museum: the view from the top is well worth the climb (156 steps).

Right: Lansdown Tower, seen from the cemetery.

Kingswood School, on Lansdown Road, was opened by John Wesley in 1748 at Kingswood, Bristol, and transferred to Bath in 1852. Initially entrance was restricted to sons of Methodist preachers, and the regime was Spartan. Pupils got up at five in the morning and went to bed at eight at night, without any playtime. The new school, by the architect James Wilson, was erected in Perpendicular Gothic style in the shape of an H. The building has been adapted to the needs of the time with modern classrooms, laboratories and a swimming bath, and there are now some girl pupils.

In 1820 the medieval manor of Claverton was replaced by a mansion commanding sweeping views of the Avon valley, designed by Sir Jeffrey Wyatville, architect to George IV. It is now renowned as the only comprehensive museum of Americana in Europe. Whole rooms have been re-created, using authentic original materials shipped over from America. In the 'keeping room' of a Puritan family, the beams and floorboards come from a late-17th-century house in Massachusetts, and the table belonged to Peregrine White, who was born in Cape Cod harbour aboard the *Mayflower* in 1620. There is a whaling ship, evoking the era of Moby Dick, and a beehive oven where genuine American gingerbread is baked. The garden duplicates George Washington's private garden at Mount Vernon by the Potomac River, which he developed from seeds and plants sent him by an admiring Somerset family. The parlour from the home of William Perley (1763) illustrates the American fashion of painting panelling to imitate marble textures and superior wood graining (here, cedar). The furniture is in the style which the English call Queen Anne, but which reached America later in the 18th century and continued to be popular there after it had been superseded in England. Captain Perley commanded the Boxford (Mass.) Minute Men at Bunker Hill.

Left: Kingswood School. Below: The Perley Parlor in the American Museum in Britain.

The Kennet and Avon Canal, completed in 1810, is 75 miles long and pursues a beautiful course from Reading to Bath, where it links the Thames to the Avon. The Kennet and Avon Trust is making it navigable once more, and there are idyllic walks to be had along the towpath.

Widcombe, which now virtually adjoins Bath to the south, has a perfect ensemble of church, manor house, crescent and terrace that epitomises all Bath's charms, in proportion to the village setting, on the edge of verdant countryside. The south front of Widcombe Manor (shown here) is very ornate, with fluted pilasters ending in foliated Ionic capitals, a garlanded tympanum with a central oval light and balustrading decorated with urns. Doric columns frame the entrance, and grotesque masks peer from the keystones of the windows. The bronze fountain in the courtyard is said to have come from the Palazzo Grimani in Venice. The house was remodelled in about 1727 for its owner Phillip Bennet, a Member of Parliament for Bath. The architect is not definitely known but, as Ison says, a cultivated mind was clearly at work. In the cellars, the Rotork Engineering Company started out – later to become one of Bath's most efficient industrial enterprises. Bennet was a friend of the novelist Henry Fielding and his sister Sarah, who lived nearby at Widcombe Lodge. In Widcombe churchyard, the poet Walter Savage Landor (1775–1864) would muse and brood. He was buried on a hilltop in Florence, but in one of his poems he wrote: 'Widcombe! few seek in thee their resting-place, / Yet I, when I have run my weary race, / Will throw my bones upon thy churchyard turf.'

Left: The Kennet and Avon Canal. Above: Widcombe Manor.

'The natural beauties of wood, water, and prospect, hill and dale, wilderness and cultivation,' wrote one observer of Prior Park, 'make it one of the most delightful spots I ever saw.' The ancient owners of the land were the priors of Bath, but the mansion, set on the heights of Combe Down, dates from 1735, when Ralph Allen, having amassed a fortune from his postal and quarrying enterprises, employed John Wood the elder to design a suitable architectural frame for his achievements. Allen was a modest man, but he enjoyed full-blown Palladianism, which here reaches its apogee. The principal front, to the north, displays a huge portico of giant Corinthian columns with stone balustrades filling the interstices, while the south front has another grand pedimented entrance with engaged Ionic half-columns. The grounds are naturally dramatic; as Wood said in his *Essay*, 'The Combe . . . terminates itself in the Shape of the Head of a vast Niche, with natural Terrasses rising above one another, like the Stages between the Seats of a Roman Theatre . . .'. In the valley, the fishponds are spanned by a delightful bridge, built in about 1755 and based on the bridge crossing the Nadder at Wilton House. At Prior Park Allen dispensed his hospitality to the fullest. Here he entertained such luminaries as Fielding and Pope; the novelist gave him a full-length portrait in *Tom Jones* as the beneficent Squire Allworthy, and the poet immortalised him in a neat couplet: 'Let humble Allen, with an awkward shame, / Do good by stealth, and blush to find it fame.' Allen died in 1764, and the great mansion seemed to fade with him, for his only son had died, and his second wife died after him childless. After passing through various hands, it became a seminary in 1829, and it is now a co-educational Catholic school.

Above: The north front and east pavilion of Prior Park.
Right: Prior Park's Palladian bridge, seen from the house.

Some Famous Residents

As one walks around Bath, it is difficult to avoid thinking that everyone who was famous in the 18th century lived here at some stage in their lives, there is such a wealth of commemorative plaques.

Beau Nash's contribution to the life of the city has been described above, pp. 14–17. Anecdotes abound concerning his eventful career. The best is his riposte to a coffee-house gossip who referred to the Master of Ceremonies as a whoremonger: 'I acknowledge I have a woman living in my house, but if I do keep her, a man can be no more termed a whoremonger for having one whore in the house than a cheesemonger for having one cheese.'

The great novelist Jane Austen (1775–1817) stayed at various houses in Bath, but longest at 4 Sydney Place (see overleaf), to which her family moved when her father, the Rev. George Austen, retired from his Hampshire parish. Jane Austen herself disliked Bath so much that she fainted when she heard that they were going to live there. None of her letters survive from her years at Sydney Place (1801–4) – regrettably, because this was also the time when, on a family visit to Devon, she met and was attracted to one of the few men whom her niece Cassandra ever thought worthy of her, but who tragically died just as they had begun to fall in love. Though she was unhappy and bored at Bath, in her novels the city is full of life, immortalised by her acute wit and powers of observation.

The Linley family lived in the Royal Crescent, from which Elizabeth dramatically eloped with Sheridan (see p. 65). Thomas Linley was director of concerts in Bath from the mid 1750s to the mid 1770s, and his reputation as a teacher was borne out by the prodigious accomplishments of his own children. *The New Grove's Dictionary of Music* has entries for five of them. Elizabeth and Mary were noted sopranos, appearing in London and at the Three Choirs Festival as well as in Bath. Thomas junior was 'one of the most precocious composers and performers that have been known in England'; Ozias studied the organ with the Bath organist and astronomer William Herschel (see p. 57); and William, between Civil Service postings in India, shared the management of Drury Lane Theatre with his brother-in-law Sheridan. The family was painted by both Reynolds and Gainsborough.

Of all the painters who installed themselves in Bath, it was Thomas Gainsborough who achieved the widest fame. He came to the town on the advice of his biographer–patron, Phillip Thicknesse, and began painting portraits at five guineas a time. This was in 1759, but a few years later his energy and talents were commanding far larger sums – as much as 100 guineas for a full-length portrait. His *Return from the Harvest* owed its origin to the trustworthy local carrier Wiltshire, who provided Gainsborough with free transport. 'No, no,' he protested, when the artist offered him money, 'I love painting too much.' Gainsborough pressed him to accept payment and Wiltshire replied, 'When you think that I have carried to the value of a little painting, I beg you will let me have one, sir, and I shall be more than paid.' Gainsborough set about the painting, incorporating the carrier's wagon and horse in the composition.

Right: Famous residents. Above: left, Elizabeth Linley, an engraving after Gainsborough; right, Beau Nash by William Hoare. Below: left, Ralph Allen by Thomas Hudson; right, Jane Austen, the engraving for Austen-Leigh's Memoir from the drawing by her sister Cassandra.

Fanny Burney, author of *Evelina* and daughter of the music historian Charles Burney, lived with her French émigré husband General d'Arblay at 14 South Parade, where, as she said, 'there is always the town at command and always the country for prospect, exercise and delight'. *Evelina*, a novel detailing the dalliance and intrigues of another fashionable spa – Hotwells, Bristol – came out in 1778, when Fanny Burney was only 25, and was a runaway success; Sir Joshua Reynolds had to be fed while reading it, and Edmund Burke sat up all night absorbing its finer points. A playful passage in her diary describes Fanny Burney's visit with Mrs Thrale (Mrs Piozzi) to an alderman of Bath, Mr Ferry, and pokes gentle fun at the fashion for mechanical novelty which was beginning to beset Regency England.

'We perceived through a glass', she says, 'a perspective view of ships, boats and water. This raree show over, the maid who officiated as show-woman had a hint given her, and presently a trap-door opened and up jumped a covered table ornamented with various devices. When we had expressed our delight at this long enough to satisfy Mr Ferry, another hint was given, and presently down dropped an eagle from the ceiling whose talons were put into a certain hook at the top of the covering of the table, and when the admiration at this was over, up again flew the eagle, conveying in his talons the cover, and leaving under it a repast of cakes, sweetmeats, oranges and jellies.'

Left: Fanny Burney's House, 14 South Parade. Above: Part of Sydney Place. Jane Austen lived at no. 4.

Oliver Goldsmith (1730–74) is one of our primary sources for information about 18th-century Bath. In his biography of Beau Nash, he describes the growth of the town from a place affording rural pleasures and company that was 'splenetic, rustic and vulgar' to a resort for the aristocratic, cultivated and wealthy. He was a great literary all-rounder, famous equally for a play (*She Stoops to Conquer*), a poem (*The Traveller*) and a novel (*The Vicar of Wakefield*). Dr Johnson observed of him that 'No man was more foolish when he had not a pen in hand, or more wise when he had.'

No. 8 Gay Street is known as the Carved House, because the lintels are worked with garlands draped round the capitals of the Corinthian pilasters, perhaps demonstrating the taste of the first leaseholder, the painter William Hoare (his portrait of Beau Nash is reproduced on p. 91). Later it was the home of Mrs Piozzi, erstwhile friend of the great lexicographer Dr Johnson. He broke the connection when she married Mr Piozzi, an Italian musician,

after the death of her first husband, Mr Thrale. She settled in Gay Street in 1816, and on her 80th birthday gave a party at the Assembly Rooms at which she danced 'with astonishing elasticity' until the early morning.

St James's Square, unusual in that streets lead off its corners at oblique angles, was built at the end of the 18th century on gardens and orchards of the Royal Crescent residents, much to their annoyance. At no. 35 lived the poet and critic Walter Savage Landor (1775–1864). A mixture of generosity and cantankerousness, Landor achieved a literary reputation after being expelled from Oxford (for firing a gun at a Tory student) and fighting for the Spanish against the French in the Peninsular War. He met his wife in 1811 at a ball in Bath and promptly decided, 'That's the nicest girl in the room and I'll marry her.' The marriage endured remarkably well, considering his disputatious character, only falling apart completely in 1835, when he left Mrs Landor in Fiesole and settled in Bath.

Homes of the famous. Above left, 11 North Parade, at one time a lodging house. Here stayed Oliver Goldsmith, poet, playwright, novelist, and biographer of the famous Master of Ceremonies Beau Nash. It was also the residence of the statesman Edmund Burke (1729–97), during his final illness. Above right, 8 Gay Street, the home at different times of Prince Hoare, the painter, and Dr Johnson's old acquaintance Mrs Piozzi. Right, 17 The Circus, where Gainsborough lived. Left, 35 St James's Square, home of the poet Landor, who was visited here both by the historian Thomas Carlyle and by Charles Dickens. The novelist put Bath into his *Pickwick Papers* (1836) with his particular gift for transforming the familiar into the comically strange – as when Mr Pickwick and his friends declare Park Street to be 'very much like the perpendicular street a man sees in a dream, which he cannot get up for the life of him'.

BATH: THE HISTORIC CENTRE

KEY

1 Abbey Church of St Peter & St Paul
2 Tourist Information Centre
3 Grand Pump Room
4 Concert Room
5 Roman Baths
6 Roman Baths Museum
7 Burrows Toy Museum
8 Ralph Allen's House
9 Sally Lunn's House
10 Abbey Church House
11 St John's Hospital
12 Cross Bath
13 Theatre Royal
14 Beau Nash's House
15 Royal Mineral Water Hospital
16 General Wolfe's House
17 Octagon
18 Postal Museum
19 Post Office
20 City Library & Victoria Art Gallery
21 Market
22 Guildhall

P Parking
--- Pedestrianised areas
➤ One way system

0 ————— 100

YARDS

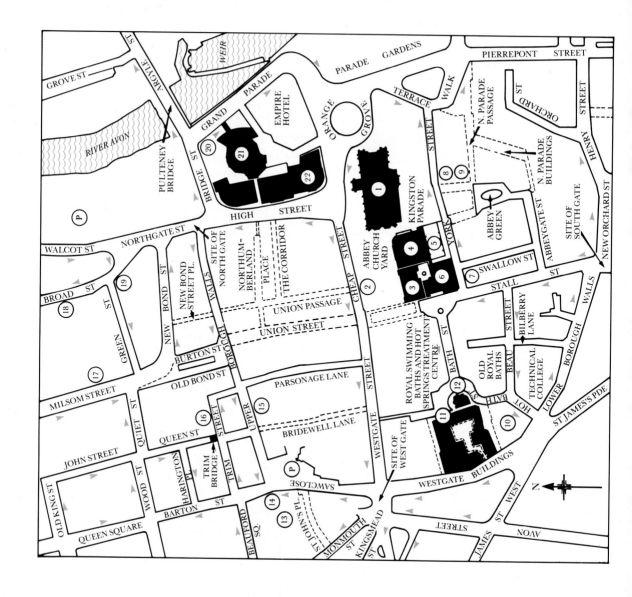